INDEX

Conquering Exam Stress: Proven Techniques from a Therapist

Donna Morgan

Course Objective: To provide students with practical tools and techniques to manage and overcome exam stress, improve their mental wellbeing and enhance their academic performance.

Hello and welcome to the paperback version of Conquering Exam Stress: A Comprehensive Guide to Mastering Your Mind and Achieving Success - written by me, Donna Morgan. I'm so glad you've decided to join me on this journey towards better understanding and managing the stress that comes along with exams.

We've all been there—sitting in a quiet room, feeling the weight of a thousand thoughts and fears pressing down on us as we try to focus on the questions in front of us. Exam stress is a universal experience, but that doesn't mean we have to let it control us. In this book, I'll share practical tips, personal experiences and expert insights to help you overcome the pressure and achieve success in your exams.

INTRODUCTION

Welcome to "Conquer Exam Stress: Proven Techniques from a Therapist," a comprehensive course designed to equip you with practical tools and techniques to manage and overcome exam stress, improve your mental wellbeing and enhance your academic performance.

As your instructor, my name is Donna Morgan and I have over 27 years of experience working within schools as a counsellor specialising in supporting adolescents with exam stress. Throughout my career I have helped countless students navigate the challenges of exam stress and have developed a deep understanding of the issues they face.

In this course, we will delve into the science of stress and its impact on the mind and body. You will learn practical stress management techniques, develop effective time management and study skills and understand the importance of a balanced lifestyle for overall well-being. Additionally, we will focus on building resilience, coping strategies and preparing for exam day.

Let's get started......

CHAPTER ONE

Understanding exam stress: Causes, symptoms and consequences

Exam stress is a prevalent and significant concern for students across the globe. In this section, we will explore the nature of exam stress, the reasons behind its occurrence and the various ways it impacts students. By gaining a deeper understanding of this phenomenon, we can better equip ourselves to manage and mitigate its effects.

Exam stress, at its core, is a state of tension or anxiety that arises in anticipation of or during examinations. It is a response to the pressures and demands associated with these high-stakes academic events, which can have considerable consequences for a student's academic standing and future opportunities.

There are multiple factors that contribute to the emergence of exam stress. One primary factor is the weight of expectations, both from oneself and from others, such as parents, teachers or peers. Performance anxiety, the fear of not meeting these expectations, can exacerbate the stress experienced by students.

Additionally, time constraints and the sheer volume of material to be mastered for exams can further intensify feelings of anxiety.

The effects of exam stress manifest differently in each individual. For some students, it may present as a mild, transient sensation of unease that serves as a motivating force. However, for others, it can escalate into a debilitating state of panic that negatively impacts their mental, emotional and physical well-being. It is crucial to recognise and address these diverse manifestations in order to support students effectively.

Symptoms of exam stress may include anxiety, irritability, difficulty concentrating, sleep disturbances and even physical symptoms like headaches and stomach aches.

If not managed effectively, exam stress can negatively impact a student's mental health, academic performance and overall well-being.

In this course, we will explore practical strategies to address the root causes of exam stress and learn how to manage its effects, allowing you to perform at your best during exams and beyond.

Now that we've established what exam stress is and why it pops up like an unwanted pimple on picture day, it's time to dive into the strategies and tools that can help tame this academic beast.

In the next section, where we'll explore ways to keep exam stress at bay – or at least confine it to the corner, where it can sulk in solitude.

Stress and the Mind-Body Connection

Welcome to the fascinating world of stress! Did you know that stress can be both a hero and a villain in our lives? It's true! When we face challenges, stress can help us mobilise our resources and sharpen our focus. But when it overstays its welcome, it can wreak havoc on our minds and bodies.

When we experience stress, our bodies produce hormones such as adrenaline and cortisol. These hormones prepare our bodies for the famous "fight or flight" response, which was super useful back in the caveman days when we had to dodge sabre-toothed tigers. However, in modern times, the tigers have been replaced by exams and our bodies still respond as if we're in physical danger.

So, how does stress impact our academic performance?

Well, imagine trying to solve a maths problem while being chased by a hungry bear. Not easy, right? That's how our brains feel when we're trying to learn or perform under stress.

When stress levels are moderate, it can actually improve our attention and focus. But when stress becomes chronic or too intense, it can impair our memory, concentration and overall cognitive functioning. In other words, too much stress can turn our brains into mush – not exactly ideal for acing that exam!

The key to success lies in striking the perfect balance. We'll learn how to harness the power of stress while keeping it at bay, so it doesn't transform into an unruly beast gnawing at our academic dreams.

As we've mentioned before, stress can act as both a friend and a foe. When it comes to academic performance, a moderate amount of stress can actually sharpen our minds, boosting our concentration and alertness.

However, when stress levels are too high or persistent, it can create a barrier to learning and hinder our academic achievements such as:

Memory problems: High stress levels can interfere with our ability to encode, store and retrieve information, making it difficult to remember what we've studied.

Difficulty concentrating: Overwhelming stress can make it hard for us to focus on the task at hand, which can negatively affect our learning and test-taking abilities.

Decreased motivation: Chronic stress can sap our energy and enthusiasm for learning, resulting in a lack of motivation to study and complete assignments.

Test anxiety: Excessive stress can cause test anxiety, which may lead to poor test performance, even if we know the material well.

Procrastination: When we're stressed, we may find ourselves putting off important tasks, leading to a cycle of procrastination that can harm our academic progress.

Impaired problem-solving and decision-making: Stress can hinder our ability to think critically, solve problems and make effective decisions, all of which are essential skills for academic success.

Physical health consequences: Prolonged stress can lead to physical health issues, such as headaches, sleep disturbances, and weakened immune systems, which can further impact our ability to perform well academically.

In conclusion, this chapter has provided an overview of exam stress and its impact on students' academic performance and well-being. As we move forward, we will explore effective strategies for combating exam stress, including adopting healthy lifestyles and developing good study habits and time management skills.

CHAPTER TWO

Identifying personal stress triggers and stress responses

We're all unique and our stress triggers are no exception. What might cause one person to feel overwhelmed could be a walk in the park for someone else.

To conquer exam stress, it's crucial to identify your personal stress triggers and recognise your stress responses.

Identifying stress patterns can help you defuse stress before it escalates.

It's essential to pay attention to your thoughts, emotions and physical responses when you're feeling stressed.

Do you get headaches or stomach aches?

Do you find yourself procrastinating or doubting your abilities?

By recognising your patterns, you can defuse stress before it escalates.

Exam stress triggers can vary from person to person and can include fear of failure, time management issues, perceived difficulty or lack of preparation.

To identify your unique triggers, take some time to reflect on past exam experiences and what caused you anxiety.

Once you've identified your triggers, it's time to observe how your body and mind respond to stress.

Common responses are;

Physical symptoms such as headaches or stomach aches.

Emotional reactions such as irritability or anxiety.

Cognitive signs like negative thoughts or self-doubt.

Behavioural responses like procrastination or social withdrawal.

By becoming aware of your unique stress responses, you can monitor yourself during exam periods and take action to manage your stress levels more effectively.

Cognitive Behavioural Therapy (CBT) is an evidence-based approach that can be helpful in managing exam stress triggers.

In this chapter, we will explore how CBT can be applied to identify and manage your unique stress triggers.

First, it's essential to recognise that our thoughts and beliefs about exam situations can influence how we feel and behave. This is known as the cognitive triad in CBT - the interconnected relationship between our thoughts, emotions and behaviours.

By understanding this relationship, we can start to identify and challenge any negative thoughts and beliefs that may be contributing to our exam stress.

To begin, take some time to reflect on past exam experiences and identify any negative thoughts or beliefs that may have contributed to your stress levels. For example, you might have had thoughts such as "I'll never pass this exam" or "I'm not smart enough." These thoughts can be automatic and difficult to challenge, but they can contribute to feelings of anxiety and stress.

Once you have identified your negative thoughts and beliefs, it's time to challenge them.

Ask yourself if there is any evidence to support these thoughts. Are they based on facts or assumptions?

Are there alternative ways of looking at the situation that might be more realistic?

Next, it's important to develop positive coping strategies that are based on your newfound understanding of your stress triggers. This might include developing positive self-talk, breaking down tasks into smaller, manageable chunks or seeking social support when you need it.

Let's consider the following example of a vicious cycle that someone may experience when facing exam stress:

Trigger: The thought of an upcoming exam.
Negative thought: "I'm going to fail this exam and it will ruin my academic career."

Emotion: Anxiety, fear and hopelessness.

Behaviour: Procrastination, avoidance and withdrawal.

Consequence: Inadequate preparation and decreased confidence, leading to a lower exam score and further reinforcement of negative beliefs.

To change this vicious cycle, we can apply the CBT model by:

Identifying and challenging the negative thought: "I'm going to fail this exam, and it will ruin my academic career."

Evidence for: I've struggled with this subject before and I don't feel confident in my abilities.

Evidence against: I have prepared for this exam by studying the material and I have passed exams in this subject before.

Alternative thought: "I have prepared for this exam and I will do my best. Even if I don't perform as well as I hoped, it won't ruin my academic career."

Positive self-talk: "I am capable and prepared for this exam."

Time management: Breaking down the material into manageable chunks and creating a study schedule.

Seeking social support: Talking to friends or family members for encouragement and motivation.

By applying these CBT techniques, you can break the vicious cycle of exam stress and negative beliefs.

By challenging negative thoughts, developing positive coping strategies and building resilience, you can take control of your exam stress and achieve success in your academic pursuits.

CHAPTER THREE

Practical Stress Management Techniques
Breathing

Breathing exercises for instant stress relief

Take a deep breath – no, seriously, try it right now. Doesn't that feel better? Breathing exercises are like a secret weapon against stress. When we're anxious or stressed, our breathing tends to become shallow and rapid. But by consciously taking slow, deep breaths, we can signal our brains to chill out.

Throughout this chapter, we'll explore various breathing exercises that you can use to keep stress at bay. Keep practising them, come back to this chapter when needed. The more you practise, the more your body will thank you and remember 'oh it's that calming down trick!"

They are perfect for those times when you need a quick and discreet way to regain your composure – because let's face it, busting out yoga poses in the middle of the library might not be the most practical solution.

The 7/11 Technique:

The 7/11 technique is a calming breathing method that helps students relax during moments of stress. It's as simple as buying your favourite snack at the corner store! Just follow these steps: If you practise this it will work, its my favourite technique of all. I practise it everyday. Once your mind and body know this technique they will always know it. The 7/11 is your instant anytime any place technique

- Sit or stand comfortably, and take a moment to notice how you feel.
- Inhale slowly and deeply through your nose for a count of 7. Imagine you're filling your lungs with fresh air and positive energy.
- Now, exhale slowly through your mouth for a count of 11.like your blowing through a straw As you do this, picture all your stress and worries leaving your body.
- Repeat this process for a few minutes or until you start to feel calmer.

Remember, practice makes perfect – just like your exam revision!

Square Box Breathing:

Square box breathing is a simple technique that's as easy as drawing a box (well, almost). Give this method a try and see how it helps you find your zen:

- Sit or stand comfortably with a straight back and relaxed shoulders.
- Picture a square box in your mind, and imagine you're going to trace its outline with your breath.
- Inhale slowly through your nose counting in 2 3 4, tracing the first side of the box.

- Hold your breath for another count of hold 2 3 4 as you trace the second side.
- Exhale slowly through your mouth out 2 3 4, completing the third side.
- Hold your breath again for a count of hold 2 3 4, finishing the final side of the square.
- Repeat this process 4-5 times or until you feel more relaxed and focused.

It's like a bit of mental doodling for your brain!

The "Belly Laughs" Breathing Technique:

This third technique adds a touch of humour to help you lighten up and reduce stress. After all, laughter is the best medicine, right?

- Sit or stand comfortably, placing one hand on your chest and the other on your belly.
- Take a slow, deep breath through your nose, focusing on making your belly rise (rather than your chest).
- As you exhale through your mouth, let out a gentle, fake laugh (think "ha-ha-ha" or "hee-hee-hee").
- Continue this process for a few minutes, gradually increasing the volume and enthusiasm of your laughter. You might just find that your fake laughter turns into genuine giggles!
- When you're finished, take a few slow, deep breaths and notice how much lighter and more relaxed you feel.

Try these techniques during your study breaks or before an exam and see how much more relaxed and focused you become. Remember, a calm mind is a powerful tool for tackling even the toughest exam questions!

CHAPTER FOUR

Mindfulness and meditation techniques to cultivate calmness

Mindfulness and meditation are like the superheroes of stress management. With their powers combined, they can help you achieve a state of Zen-like calmness even when exams loom large on the horizon. Like the breathing techniques, come back to this chapter for instant calmness.

Mindfulness teaches us to be present in the moment, embracing our thoughts and feelings without judgement. Meditation, on the other hand, helps us find our inner sanctuary, where we can escape the chaos of everyday life for a moment of peace.

Together, we'll explore various mindfulness and meditation techniques that will help you stay grounded, focused and centred – even when it feels like your to-do list is longer than the Harry Potter series.

Here are three mindfulness techniques to help students achieve instant calmness during exam stress. These techniques should be well practised for when you need to implement them when needed.

The "5-4-3-2-1" Sensory Countdown:

This technique helps you ground yourself in the present moment by focusing on your senses. It's a firm personal favourite of mine, Plus, it's as easy as counting down from five – no rocket science degree required!

- Sit or stand comfortably and take a deep breath.
- Look around and name (silently or out loud) five things you can see. Maybe it's your colourful study notes, a lucky mascot, or that pile of clothes you've been meaning to wash.
- Next, identify four things you can hear. It could be the sound of your own breathing, birds chirping outside, or your neighbour's questionable taste in music.
- Now, find three things you can touch. Feel the texture of your desk, the smoothness of a pen, or the warmth of your favourite hoodie.
- Moving on, identify two things you can smell. Perhaps it's the scent of your freshly brewed coffee or the aroma of your favourite stress-relief candle.
- Finally, pinpoint one thing you can taste. Maybe it's the lingering taste of your last snack, or you can simply pop a mint or piece of gum into your mouth.
- Take a deep breath and appreciate how this quick sensory countdown has brought you back to the present moment.

Just like that, you've escaped the stress spiral without even leaving your desk!

The "Gratitude-itude" Technique:

This mindfulness technique helps you shift your focus from stress to gratitude, reminding you that there's more to life than exams. After all, what's the point of acing an exam if you can't appreciate the little things?

- Sit or stand comfortably and take a deep breath to centre yourself.
- Close your eyes and take a moment to think of three things you're grateful for today. They can be as simple or as profound as you like – maybe it's the sunny weather, a supportive friend, or that extra cookie you sneaked in at lunch.
- For each thing you're grateful for, say (silently or out loud), "Thank you, [insert gratitude item here], for making my day brighter."
- Take a few moments to really feel the appreciation and warmth that gratitude brings. Picture each gratitude item like a warm, fuzzy blanket, wrapping around you and shielding you from exam stress.
- Once you've finished, take another deep breath and open your eyes. Notice how much lighter and more positive you feel.

The "Stealthy Toe Tapper" Technique:

This technique can be used on exam day, as no-one will know you are doing it. It's instant calm! It helps you regain focus and alleviate stress by grounding yourself through subtle physical sensations. It's so sneaky, even secret agents would be impressed!

- Sit comfortably in your exam chair, keeping your back straight and your feet flat on the floor.
- Take a moment to notice how you're feeling and acknowledge any stress or anxiety.
- Begin to gently and slowly tap your right big toe on the floor, keeping your foot flat. Tap it about five times, focusing your full attention on the sensation of your toe touching the floor.
- Now, switch to your left big toe and do the same thing – gently tap it on the floor about five times, concentrating on the sensation.
- Continue to alternate between your right and left big toes, tapping each one a few times, and letting the simple, repetitive motion ground you in the present moment.
- As you tap, remind yourself that stress is a natural part of the exam process, but by focusing on the task at hand, you can overcome it.
- Once you feel more relaxed and focused, stop tapping and bring your attention back to your exam.

The "Stealthy Toe Tapper" technique is so subtle that no one will even notice you're doing it. You'll be like a stress-fighting ninja, conquering exams one toe tap at a time!

By incorporating this discreet mindfulness technique during exams, students can regain their focus, reduce anxiety, and perform at their best – all without raising any eyebrows.

CHAPTER FIVE

Visualisation exercises

Visualisation exercises for mental preparation and focus.
Imagine yourself sitting in the exam room, pencil in hand, confidently answering every question with ease. Now, what if we told you that just picturing this scenario could actually improve your chances of making it a reality?

Visualisation exercises act as delightful mental rehearsals for those grand moments when the spotlight is on you. By playfully imagining your triumph in the face of challenges, you're not only giving your brain a pep talk, but you're also getting it ready for the main event.

"Stress-Busting Balloon" Technique:

This visualisation exercise helps you release stress and anxiety by imagining that you're filling a balloon with your worries and then letting them float away. It's like sending your stress on a one-way trip to the stratosphere!

- Find a comfortable place to sit or lie down, away from any distractions.
- Close your eyes and take a few deep breaths, inhaling through your nose and exhaling through your mouth.

- Picture a deflated balloon in your mind. It can be any colour or shape you like. This is your "Stress-Busting Balloon."
- Now, imagine that with each exhale, you're filling the balloon with all your stress, anxiety, and worries related to exams. Visualise these negative emotions as a grey mist or smoke, flowing from your body into the balloon.
- As the balloon fills up, notice how your body and mind feel lighter and more relaxed.
- Once the balloon is full, imagine tying it off securely, ensuring that all your stress and anxiety are contained within.
- Now, visualise releasing the balloon into the sky. Watch as it floats higher and higher, carrying your stress and worries away from you.
- As the balloon becomes a tiny speck in the distance, take a moment to appreciate the lightness and calmness you feel.
- Take a few more deep breaths, and then slowly open your eyes, feeling refreshed and ready to tackle your exams with a clear mind.

"Mental Oasis" Technique

This visualisation exercise helps you create a peaceful, relaxing sanctuary in your mind, providing a temporary escape from exam stress.

- Find a comfortable place to sit or lie down, away from any distractions.
- Close your eyes and take a few deep breaths, inhaling through your nose and exhaling through your mouth.

- Picture a calming and peaceful place in your mind. This could be a beautiful beach, a serene forest, or even a cosy room filled with your favourite things. This is your "Mental Oasis."
- Begin to explore this space in your mind, noticing the sights, sounds, and smells around you. Immerse yourself in the tranquil atmosphere.
- As you spend time in your Mental Oasis, allow your stress and anxiety to melt away. Feel your body and mind becoming more relaxed and at ease.
- Spend a few minutes in this space, enjoying the sense of peace and calm it brings.
- When you're ready, take a few more deep breaths and then gently open your eyes, returning to the present moment feeling refreshed and rejuvenated.

The "Future Success" Technique

This visualisation exercise helps you build confidence and reduce exam stress by imagining yourself succeeding in your exams and achieving your goals.

- Find a comfortable place to sit or lie down, away from any distractions.
- Close your eyes and take a few deep breaths, inhaling through your nose and exhaling through your mouth.
- Begin to imagine a future version of yourself who has successfully completed your exams. Picture this future self as confident, happy, and accomplished.

- As you visualise your future self, notice the feelings of pride, joy, and satisfaction that come with your success. Let these positive emotions fill your body and mind.
- Now, imagine your future self giving you advice and encouragement. What would they say? Perhaps they'd remind you to believe in yourself, take breaks, or ask for help when needed.
- Spend a few moments absorbing the wisdom and support from your future self, feeling inspired and motivated.
- When you're ready, take a few more deep breaths and then gently open your eyes, returning to the present moment with a renewed sense of confidence and determination.

By practising these visualisation techniques, students can create a mental space for relaxation and encouragement, helping them to manage exam stress and maintain a calm and focused mindset.

CHAPTER SIX

Time Management and Study Skills - Setting Realistic Goals and Expectations

Effective time management and study skills are crucial for reducing exam stress and achieving academic success. In this section, we will discuss the importance of setting realistic goals and expectations.

Assess your current abilities: Before setting goals, take stock of your current knowledge and skills. Understand your strengths and weaknesses in relation to the subject matter and use this information to create a tailored study plan.

Break down larger goals: Divide your overall academic goals into smaller, more manageable tasks. For example, instead of aiming to master an entire subject, focus on specific chapters, topics or skills that you want to improve.

Set SMART goals: Make your goals Specific, Measurable, Achievable, Relevant, and Time-bound. This approach will help you create clear, attainable objectives that are aligned with your abilities and priorities.

Prioritise your tasks: Determine the most important and urgent tasks in your study plan, and allocate your time and energy accordingly. Focus on completing high-priority tasks first, and avoid getting bogged down in less critical details.

Create a study schedule: Develop a consistent study routine that takes into account your goals, priorities and personal commitments. Be sure to include regular breaks and allocate time for self-care, as these activities are essential for maintaining focus and reducing stress.

Monitor your progress: Periodically review your goals and track your achievements. Celebrate small victories along the way and adjust your expectations as needed. Remember that learning is a dynamic process and it's normal to encounter setbacks or obstacles.

Seek support: Don't hesitate to reach out to teachers, classmates or tutors for assistance in achieving your goals. They can provide valuable guidance, encouragement and resources to help you stay on track.

Embrace flexibility: Life is unpredictable and sometimes circumstances may require you to adapt your goals or study plans. Be open to change and willing to reevaluate your expectations as necessary.

By setting realistic goals and expectations, you can develop effective time management and study skills that will not only help you manage exam stress but also lay the foundation for lifelong learning and personal growth.

How to use SMART

SMART goals are an effective approach to goal-setting, particularly when it comes to managing exam stress. The acronym SMART stands for Specific, Measurable, Achievable, Relevant and Time-bound. Let's break down each component and provide examples related to exam preparation:

Specific: Your goals should be clear and well-defined, rather than vague or ambiguous. This helps you focus your efforts and avoid confusion.

Example: Instead of setting a goal like "study more for the maths exam," a specific goal would be "complete three chapters of the maths textbook each week."

Measurable: Goals should include criteria to track progress and determine when they have been achieved. This allows you to monitor your progress and stay motivated. Consider maintaining a record of your study sessions, noting specifics such as "30 minutes spent on English." On the day of the exam, tally up your total study time for that subject; you may be pleasantly surprised.

This knowledge fosters a sense of composure, reinforcing the idea that you're well-prepared and have invested a significant amount of time in your studies.
Here's a clever tactic to boost your confidence: for illustration purposes, let's assume you've attended

school for 12 years, learning English three times a week. Calculate the total time spent on English by multiplying the number of sessions per week by the number of weeks per year, then multiply by the total years (3 x 40 x 12). In this example, you would have devoted 1,440 hours to English. Add in any additional hours spent on focused revision, say, another 30. When self-doubt inevitably creeps in, remind yourself of the extensive time invested in your studies, providing a solid foundation to tackle any challenge.

Remember you have done approx 1,445 hours of english - you've got this.

Example: "Improve my maths quiz scores by 10% within four weeks" is a measurable goal, as you can compare your quiz scores before and after the set period.

Achievable: Goals should be realistic and attainable, given your current abilities, resources and constraints. Setting unrealistic goals can lead to disappointment and increased stress.

Example: If you struggle with maths, setting a goal to become a top-performing student in just a few weeks may not be achievable. Instead, aim for a more realistic goal, such as improving your maths grade by one grade.

Relevant: Your goals should align with your broader academic objectives and personal values. This helps to ensure that your efforts are focused on meaningful and worthwhile pursuits.

Example: If you plan to major in a field that requires strong maths skills, setting a goal to improve your maths performance is relevant to your long-term success.

Time-bound: Goals should have a specific deadline or time frame, which creates a sense of urgency and helps you stay committed to your objectives.

Example: "Finish reviewing all maths chapters two weeks before the exam" is a time-bound goal that encourages you to maintain a consistent study schedule.

By creating SMART goals for your studies, you can focus your efforts, track your progress, and ultimately achieve greater success in your exams.

CHAPTER SEVEN

Creating an effective study schedule

There's a famous saying: "Failing to plan is planning to fail." When it comes to exam preparation, a well-organised study schedule is your secret weapon against procrastination, all-nighters and last-minute panic.

A well-designed study schedule can make a significant difference in your exam preparation, enabling you to manage your time efficiently, maintain focus and reduce stress. In this section, we will provide a detailed guide on creating an effective study schedule.

Assess your current commitments: Begin by taking stock of your daily and weekly obligations, such as school, work, family responsibilities and social activities. This will help you understand how much time you have available for studying and identify any potential conflicts.

Determine your study priorities: Based on the subjects and topics you need to cover, rank them in order of importance or difficulty. This will allow you to allocate your study time more effectively, ensuring that you devote sufficient attention to high-priority areas.

Break tasks into manageable chunks: Divide your study material into smaller, more manageable tasks or subtopics. This will make your study sessions more focused and productive, as well as create a sense of progress and accomplishment as you complete each task.

Allocate study time: Assign specific time blocks for each subject or task, taking into account your priorities and available time. Be realistic about how much you can achieve in a given time frame and avoid overloading yourself, which can lead to burnout and increased stress.

Schedule regular breaks: Incorporate short breaks into your study schedule to rest and recharge. Brief periods of relaxation can help to maintain focus, prevent fatigue, and enhance overall productivity. Take a break by walking around the garden, being outside helps to reset the mind and body connection. Do some jumping jacks, press ups or walk the dog or anyones dog! Give the brain a rest.

Plan for self-care: Include time in your schedule for activities that promote physical, mental, and emotional well-being, such as exercise, hobbies, or socialising with friends. Maintaining a healthy balance is crucial for managing stress and sustaining motivation during exam preparation.

Set aside contingency time: Unexpected events or distractions can disrupt your study plan. Reserve some buffer time in your schedule to accommodate unforeseen circumstances or to catch up on any missed study sessions.

Monitor and adjust your schedule: Regularly review your study schedule to assess your progress and make any necessary adjustments. Be flexible and willing to modify your plan as you gain a better understanding of your needs and capabilities.

Stay accountable: Share your study schedule with a friend, family member or study group to help you stay committed to your plan. This added accountability can motivate you to stick to your schedule and achieve your goals.

Establish a dedicated space for studying that is comfortable, well-lit and free from distractions. This will help you associate this area with learning and productivity, making it easier to focus when you sit down to study.

Organise your notes, textbooks and other study materials in a way that is easily accessible and logical. Consider using binders, folders, or digital tools like note-taking apps to keep everything in order. This will save you time and energy when you need to find specific information during your study sessions.

Eliminate as many distractions as possible from your study environment. This includes turning off notifications on your devices, putting your phone on silent and minimising noise and visual clutter in your workspace.

Establish clear objectives for each study session and create a study schedule to help you stay on track.

Break down larger tasks into smaller, manageable steps and allocate specific time slots for each topic or subject. This will help you maintain focus and prevent feelings of overwhelm.

Maintain a clean and clutter-free workspace

Keep your study area clean and clutter-free by tidying up after each session.

A clear workspace can promote mental clarity and make it easier to concentrate on your studies. If you are studying in the same room you sleep, tidy up at night or throw a blanket over your work area to establish a peaceful and calming environment at nighttime.

CHAPTER EIGHT

Maintaining a Balanced Lifestyle

The importance of sleep for stress management and cognitive function.

Whoever said, "I'll sleep when I'm dead" clearly never had to sit through an exam. Sleep is essential for managing stress and maintaining optimal cognitive function. When we're well-rested, our brains are better equipped to learn, remember and problem-solve.

We'll teach you how to get the high-quality zzz's you need to keep your brain sharp and your stress levels low. Because let's be honest: nobody wants to face an exam feeling like a zombie.

Sleep is like your brain's personal assistant, helping it sort, store and consolidate all that information you've been cramming into it. Without enough sleep, your brain might end up losing vital bits of info, which is definitely not ideal when you're trying to ace an exam.

While you snooze, your brain gets to work on essential maintenance tasks, like clearing out toxins and recharging neurotransmitters. So, skimping on sleep is like asking your brain to run a marathon with a sprained ankle – not a great plan!

A well-rested brain can focus better and make smarter decisions. When you're sleep-deprived, even simple tasks can feel impossible and you're more likely to make silly mistakes during exams.

Alright, now that we've established sleep's importance let's dive into some practical tips to help you catch more of those rejuvenating zzz's:

Stick to a sleep schedule: Try to go to bed and wake up at the same time each day, even on weekends. Consistency is key for regulating your body's internal clock, making it easier to fall asleep and wake up feeling refreshed.

Create a bedtime routine: Develop a pre-sleep ritual that signals to your brain it's time to wind down. This might include activities like reading, gentle stretching or listening to calming music.

Make your bedroom sleep-friendly: Keep your bedroom cool, dark and quiet to create the ideal sleep environment. Consider investing in blackout curtains, earplugs or a white noise machine if needed.

Limit screen time before bed: The blue light emitted by screens can interfere with your body's production of melatonin, the sleep hormone. Try to unplug from screens at least an hour before bedtime and opt for a good old-fashioned book instead.

Watch your caffeine and sugar intake: Consuming caffeine and sugar too close to bedtime can make it harder to fall asleep. Aim to cut off caffeine after lunchtime and avoid sugary snacks before hitting the hay.

Exercise during the day: Regular physical activity can help you fall asleep faster and enjoy deeper sleep. Just be sure to wrap up your workout at least a few hours before bedtime, as exercising too close to bedtime can have the opposite effect.

Practice relaxation techniques: Calming activities like deep breathing, meditation or progressive muscle relaxation can help quiet your mind and prepare your body for sleep. Give them a try and see what works best for you.

By prioritising sleep and following these practical tips, you'll be better equipped to manage exam stress and perform at your best. So, it's time to ditch those all-nighters and embrace the power of a good night's sleep. Sweet dreams!

Exercise and physical activity to combat stress

Exercise is a powerful stress-reliever and mood-booster that benefits students in numerous ways. Engaging in regular physical activity not only helps improve focus and overall well-being, but it also enhances cognitive function and memory retention. So, let's dive into more details and explore some helpful tips for staying active during intense study periods.

Find an activity you enjoy: The best exercise is the one you'll stick to, so explore different activities to find what you love. Whether it's dancing, swimming, cycling, or team sports, choose something that makes you excited to get moving.

Break a sweat in short bursts: Time constraints during exam season can make it challenging to commit to long workouts. Instead, try incorporating short bursts of exercise into your day. High-Intensity Interval Training (HIIT) or quick 10-minute workouts can provide significant benefits without eating up too much of your study time.

Engaging both the left and right brain hemispheres can enhance exam preparation by activating various cognitive functions, leading to a more holistic learning experience. And who wouldn't want their brain firing on all cylinders? So, without further ado, let's dive into some physical exercises to give your brain a well-rounded workout:

Cross-Crawl: March in place while touching your right elbow to your left knee and vice versa. This exercise encourages communication between the left and right brain hemispheres, creating a harmonious brain ballet.

Juggling: Juggling not only makes you look like the life of the party, but it also improves hand-eye coordination and activates both sides of the brain. Start with two objects and work your way up. Just make sure you're not juggling your grandmother's fine china!

Yoga: Practising yoga unites mind and body (and makes you more bendy). Poses like the Tree Pose and Eagle Pose require balance and focus, stimulating the left and right brain in a peaceful, stress-busting manner.

Now, why should we stimulate both the left and right brain? Well, the left brain is the logical, analytical powerhouse, while the right brain is the creative, intuitive maestro. By engaging both hemispheres, you're essentially inviting them to a brain party where they can mingle and collaborate, leading to enhanced learning, problem-solving and stress management. It's a win-win situation for your noggin!

Exercise with a buddy: Having a workout partner can make exercise more enjoyable and keep you accountable. Plan study breaks with a friend and get moving together. This way, you can both reap the benefits of physical activity while maintaining a social connection.

Embrace the great outdoors: Nature has a calming effect on the mind, so why not combine exercise with some fresh air? Go for a walk, hike or jog in a park or nature reserve. The combination of exercise and natural surroundings can work wonders in reducing stress levels.Walking in nature has been shown to release hormones that can positively impact mental health. Specifically, reducing levels of cortisol, a stress hormone that can contribute to anxiety and depression. Additionally, nature walks can increase levels of serotonin, a neurotransmitter linked to feelings of happiness and well-being, and exposure to sunlight can boost levels of vitamin D, which has been associated with improved mood and reduced risk of depression.

Schedule exercise into your day: Treat exercise as a non-negotiable appointment in your daily routine. By setting aside time for physical activity, you're more likely to follow through and make it a habit.

Stretch and practice yoga: Stretching and yoga not only improve flexibility and posture but can also help relax the mind and body. Take breaks to stretch or incorporate yoga sessions into your routine to unwind and refocus.

By incorporating these tips into your daily life, you'll be well on your way to sweating out stress and boosting your mood, focus, and overall well-being. Remember, staying active during exam season can make a world of difference in both your academic performance and mental health.

CHAPTER 9

Nourishment

You are what you eat – especially when it comes to managing stress and supporting brain function. Let's look at "brain food" and how to fuel your body for maximum success.

Proper nourishment plays a crucial role in maintaining optimal brain function and managing exam stress among students. A well-balanced diet can provide essential nutrients that not only support cognitive performance but also help in regulating mood and reducing anxiety. In this section, we will explore the significance of nourishing the brain and how it can aid students in coping with exam stress.

Fuelling the brain with essential nutrients

The brain, like any other organ, requires specific nutrients to function at its best. Key components of a brain-healthy diet include complex carbohydrates, healthy fats, lean proteins, vitamins, minerals and antioxidants. Consuming a balanced diet that includes these nutrients can help improve memory, focus, and overall cognitive function, giving students an advantage during exam preparation and performance.

Stabilising energy levels and blood sugar

A nourishing diet, rich in complex carbohydrates and fibre, helps maintain stable energy levels and blood sugar throughout the day. This stability can prevent energy crashes, mood swings and irritability, which are common stressors during the exam period. Foods such as whole grains, legumes, fruits and vegetables provide a steady source of energy, supporting sustained focus and concentration during study sessions and exams.

Enhancing mood and reducing anxiety

Certain nutrients, such as omega-3 fatty acids, B vitamins and magnesium, play a vital role in supporting neurotransmitter production and brain function. These nutrients can positively impact mood, reduce anxiety and promote emotional well-being, making it easier for students to cope with exam stress. Foods rich in these nutrients include fatty fish, leafy greens, nuts, seeds and whole grains.

Promoting better sleep quality

A nourishing diet can also improve sleep quality, which is essential for optimal brain function and stress management. Foods containing tryptophan, an amino acid that helps produce serotonin and melatonin, can assist in regulating the sleep-wake cycle. Examples of such foods include poultry, dairy products, nuts, and seeds. Additionally, maintaining a balanced intake of nutrients such as magnesium and calcium can support restorative sleep, further helping students manage stress during exam season.

Supporting a healthy gut-brain connection

Emerging research highlights the strong connection between gut health and brain function, emphasising the role of a nourishing diet in maintaining both.

Consuming probiotic-rich foods like yogurt, kefir, sauerkraut and kimchi can help promote a healthy gut microbiome, which in turn supports cognitive function, mood regulation, and stress resilience.

If you turn to the appendix at the back of the book, you will find a seven day meal plan of nourishing food and yummy, healthy snack ideas.

BEWARE

Imagine pulling an all-nighter, cramming for exams while chugging energy drinks and snacking on sugary treats like there's no tomorrow. while it might seem like a great way to stay *energised,* the truth is, you're setting yourself up for a wild ride of study mishaps.

Sugar highs lead to crashes and brain fog, making it hard to concentrate and ace those exams. Overloading on caffeine can lead to anxiety, jitters and sleep disruption.

Besides, bingeing on junk food and coffee means neglecting essential nutrients, causing cognitive decline and building a fragile house of cards just waiting for a gust of wind to topple it down.

So choose a balanced diet rich in brain-boosting nutrients, while keeping caffeine in check. This way, you'll maintain steady energy levels and a focused mind, making your brain – and your grades – happier.

CHAPTER TEN

Building Resilience and Coping Strategies

Developing a growth mindset and embracing failure. What do Thomas Edison, J.K. Rowling, and Michael Jordan have in common? They all experienced failure on their paths to success. Embracing a growth mindset means viewing challenges and setbacks as opportunities to learn and grow, rather than reasons to give up.

Did you know that it took Sir James Dyson a staggering 5,126 prototypes before he perfected his groundbreaking bagless vacuum cleaner? That's right, 5,126 attempts that could have easily been labelled as "failures." Instead of throwing in the towel and resigning himself to a life of vacuum bags and mediocre suction, Dyson chose to embrace these setbacks as invaluable learning opportunities.
With a growth mindset firmly in place, Dyson viewed each prototype as a stepping stone towards his ultimate goal.

Developing a growth mindset for overcoming challenges.

Do you see obstacles as insurmountable barriers or opportunities for growth?

A growth mindset is like a secret weapon that helps you face challenges head-on, embrace setbacks as learning opportunities and bounce back stronger than ever. To illustrate this point, let's dive into a few relatable examples.

The Case of the Failed Maths Test

Meet Zack, a high school student who's just received his maths test results – and he's bombed it. With a fixed mindset, Zack would sulk, give up and possibly try to convince himself that he's just "not a maths person." However, with a growth mindset, Zack recognises this failure as an opportunity to learn from his mistakes, seek extra help and come back stronger for the next test. He might even develop a newfound appreciation for the beauty of algebra!

Stumbling Through a Presentation

Picture yourself giving an important presentation at work. You've rehearsed, prepared and even picked out your lucky socks. But when the time comes, you trip over your words, mix up the slides and generally fumble your way through the entire thing. Ouch! A fixed mindset would have you wallowing in embarrassment and dreading future presentations. However, a growth mindset encourages you to reflect on what went wrong, identify areas for improvement and confidently tackle the next presentation with newfound wisdom and experience. Plus, you'll have a great story to tell at your next team-building event!

We've all been there – you put yourself out there, only to face rejection. Instead of succumbing to the

In conclusion, adopting a growth mindset can make all the difference in how you approach challenges and setbacks. By seeing failures as opportunities for growth and self-improvement, you can cultivate resilience and develop coping strategies that will serve you well in all aspects of life. So go ahead, embrace your inner Thomas Edison, J.K. Rowling, or Michael Jordan and remember that failure is just another stepping stone on the path to success

CHAPTER 11

Day of your exams and avoid last-minute cramming sessions.

Tackling a big challenge like an exam is more like running a marathon than a sprint. Just as you wouldn't simply wake up one day and run 26.2 miles without training (unless you're some sort of superhuman), it's important to approach your academic quests with the same mix of preparation and dedication, so please make sure you have read all through the other chapters before opening this one! After all, a well-prepared mind is like a well-oiled running shoe —it'll help you go the distance with a bit of pep in your step!

Preparing for exam day: Tips and tricks for success

The big day is finally here: the moment you've been preparing for, the ultimate test of your knowledge and skills. But fear not, intrepid exam-taker, for we have a treasure trove of tips and tricks to help you shine on exam day!

Establish a pre-exam routine: Developing a consistent pre-exam routine can help you feel more relaxed and focused on exam day. This might include getting a good night's sleep, eating a balanced breakfast and engaging in some light exercise or meditation to help calm your nerves.

Plan your exam day logistics: Make sure you know the exam location, start time and any specific rules or requirements. Prepare all necessary materials (e.g., pens, pencils, calculator) the night before, so you don't feel rushed or stressed on exam day.

Arrive early: Give yourself plenty of time to arrive at the exam venue, find your seat and get settled. This will help reduce stress and allow you to focus on the task at hand.

Practice relaxation techniques: If you find yourself feeling anxious or overwhelmed during the exam, take a moment to practise one of the techniques we have gone through in the previous chapters. It should be well rehearsed by now for you to immediately implement. to help calm your nerves and regain focus.

Read the exam instructions carefully: Before diving into the exam, take the time to read the instructions thoroughly. Make sure you understand the format, point values, and time limits for each section.

Prioritise your time: Allocate your time wisely during the exam. Start by tackling questions you feel confident about and move on to more challenging ones later. Keep an eye on the time to ensure you can answer all questions within the given timeframe.

Use a systematic approach: Break complex problems down into smaller, more manageable steps. This will help you work through the questions more efficiently and avoid getting overwhelmed.

Review your answers: If time permits, take a moment to review your answers before submitting your exam. Double-check your calculations, grammar and spelling, and make sure you've answered every question to the best of your ability.

Stay positive: Maintain a positive attitude throughout the exam. Remind yourself of your preparation and hard work, and trust your abilities. A positive mindset can boost your confidence and help you perform better.

Learn from your experience: After the exam, take some time to reflect on your performance. Identify areas where you did well and areas for improvement. Use this feedback to inform your study habits and test-taking strategies for future exams.

By incorporating these tips and tricks into your exam preparation, you'll be better equipped to handle the challenges of exam day. Remember, the key to success is a combination of preparation, effective test-taking strategies, and a positive mindset. With these tools at your disposal, you can face your exams with confidence and achieve the results you desire.

CHAPTER 12

Reflection

Reflecting on your journey and celebrating your achievements.

Congratulations! You've made it to the end of this stress-busting adventure. But before you ride off into the sunset, it's important to take a moment to reflect on your journey and celebrate your achievements.

In this final section, we'll guide you through a process of self-reflection, helping you to recognise your growth, acknowledge your progress and celebrate your newfound skills in managing exam stress. Remember: every step you've taken in this course is a testament to your resilience, determination, and commitment to personal growth.

Continuing your stress management journey beyond this course

As you move forward, continue to apply the strategies and techniques you've learned, refine your personalised stress management toolkit and seek out new resources and support to help you stay on track.

Remember, conquering exam stress is an ongoing process and it's important to be patient with yourself and celebrate your progress along the way. We wish you the very best in your future academic endeavours and beyond – may you continue to thrive and flourish!

The journey to mastering stress management is an ongoing one, and it is important to stay proactive in cultivating resilience and adaptability in the face of future challenges.

Keep learning and evolving: Just as stressors and life circumstances change, so too should your stress management strategies. Stay open to exploring new techniques and approaches that may better suit your evolving needs. Keep learning from books, articles, workshops, and other resources to expand your understanding of stress management and build a diverse set of coping skills.

Monitor your progress: Regularly assess your stress levels and the effectiveness of your stress management techniques. Reflect on your experiences, identify areas for improvement, and adjust your strategies accordingly. This self-awareness will help you stay in tune with your needs and make informed decisions about your well-being.

Build a support network: Surround yourself with individuals who understand your goals and can provide encouragement, guidance, and support. This may include friends, family, mentors, or mental health professionals. A strong support network can be invaluable in helping you stay motivated and accountable on your journey.

And so, dear reader, we've reached the end of our time together exploring exam stress.

I would like to thank you for joining me on this empowering journey. My hope is that the insights and tools shared in this book will serve as a valuable resource for you or your loved ones, helping to navigate the challenges of exam season with confidence and calm.

If this book has positively impacted your life or the life of someone you know, please consider sharing your experience with others. Your recommendation could make a significant difference for someone struggling with exam stress and anxiety, providing them with the support they need to achieve their goals.

As you move forward, remember the lessons learned and the techniques we've discussed. Keep practising self-care, mindfulness and effective study habits. You have the power within you to conquer exam stress and achieve the success you desire.

Warmly,

Donna x

(Dedicated to Felix, Oliver and Jasper)

EXTRA INFORMATION

Helpful tips for the papers.

Simplified Strategies for Reading Exam Questions

This section presents easy-to-understand strategies for reading exam questions, helping you comprehend and answer them correctly. Simple examples illustrate these strategies.

Active Reading: Engage with the text, identify key terms, and ask questions to clarify understanding. This helps you fully comprehend the question and answer it effectively.

Example: "Explain why recycling is important."
Steps: Read carefully, identify key terms (recycling, important), and ask relevant questions.

Breaking Down Complex Questions: Make complex questions manageable by breaking them into smaller components. Identify components, understand relationships and analyse the question's purpose.

Example: "Compare school lunches in two countries and discuss their nutritional value."

Steps: Identify components (school lunches, countries, nutritional value), understand relationships (compare lunches), analyse purpose (discuss nutritional value).

Contextualising the Question: Relate the question to course material, recognise themes and concepts, and identify potential real-world examples. This helps frame your answer in a broader context.

Example: "Discuss the effects of pollution on the environment."

Steps: Relate to course material (lectures/readings on pollution), recognise themes (environmental impact), identify real-world examples (air, water, or land pollution).

The Five W's (and One H) Approach: Answer exam questions using Who, What, Where, When, Why, and How, ensuring a comprehensive answer. Apply these questions to your exam questions and use them as a guide.

Example: "Describe the process of making a sandwich."

Five W's and How Approach: Who (person making the sandwich), What (sandwich), Where (kitchen), When (lunchtime), Why (to eat), How (steps to make the sandwich).

Inverted Pyramid Technique: Prioritise information and present your answer logically. Start with the most important details and then provide supporting information.

Example: "Explain the benefits of exercise."
Inverted Pyramid Approach: Present main argument (exercise is beneficial), provide supporting evidence (health benefits), elaborate on details (specific advantages).

Tips for Reading Exam Questions Correctly
Time Management: Allocate time for reading and understanding questions, balancing this with answering time. Monitor progress throughout the exam.

Example: A 1-hour exam with four questions:
Allocate 8 minutes for reading/understanding (2 minutes per question)
Dedicate 52 minutes to answering (13 minutes per question)

Note-Taking: Develop a system for annotating exam questions to clarify thoughts and ideas. This aids in understanding the question and guides you when crafting your response.

Example: "Discuss the benefits of teamwork."
Note-taking Steps: Underline key terms (benefits, teamwork), jot down initial thoughts (collaboration, communication), organise ideas.

Double-Checking: Review your interpretation of the question and ensure it aligns with the question's intent. Double-check your answer and make adjustments as necessary.

Example: "Explain how plants grow."
Double-checking Steps: Review interpretation (focus on plant growth), confirm alignment with the question, make adjustments as needed (add or revise details).

More often than not, people share how everything was smooth sailing until that one tricky question popped up – the party crasher of the exam world. So, why not be prepared for this uninvited guest? When you stumble upon that tough question, instead of panicking, greet it with a warm, "Ah, there you are, you cheeky rascal! I've been waiting for you." Then, leave it aside for the moment.

Focus on answering the questions you're more comfortable with first, and then circle back to tackle that pesky intruder. This approach not only adds a touch of levity to the situation but also nurtures a flexible and resilient problem-solving spirit.

Reasonable Adjustments

In the UK, reasonable adjustments are made for students with additional needs during the exam period to ensure they have equal opportunities to demonstrate their knowledge and skills. These adjustments vary depending on the student's specific needs and may include:

Extra time: Students may be granted additional time to complete their exams, typically 25% more than the standard allotted time, depending on their needs.

Rest breaks: Students may be allowed supervised rest breaks during the exam, which do not count towards the total exam time. These breaks can help students with concentration difficulties, fatigue, or other medical conditions.

Modified exam papers: Exam papers can be modified in various ways to accommodate a student's needs, such as enlarged font, modified language, or Braille transcription for visually impaired students.

Use of a reader: A reader can assist students with reading difficulties or visual impairments by reading the exam questions aloud.

Use of a scribe: A scribe can write down the student's answers if they have difficulty writing or are unable to write due to a disability.

Use of a word processor: Students may be allowed to use a word processor or computer to type their answers instead of handwriting, particularly for those with dyslexia or other writing difficulties.

Separate or alternative exam venue: Students may take exams in a separate room with fewer distractions, or alternative exam venues can be arranged for students with specific needs, such as those who require specialised equipment or support.

Prompter: A prompter can help students with attention difficulties by reminding them to stay on task and focus on the exam.

Assistive technology: Students may be allowed to use assistive technology, such as screen readers, speech-to-text software, or specialised keyboards, to help them complete the exam.
Alternative assessment methods: In some cases, alternative assessment methods, such as coursework or oral assessments, may be used in place of traditional written exams.

These adjustments are determined on a case-by-case basis and depend on the individual student's needs and the nature of their disability. Schools and examination boards work closely with students, parents, and educational professionals to ensure that appropriate support is in place during the exam period.

MEAL PLAN AND SNACKS

Here's a meal plan for a week designed to boost brain power and keep your student energised during exam season. This meal plan features UK-friendly ingredients and dishes, with a focus on nutrients that are important for cognitive function, such as omega-3 fatty acids, antioxidants, and complex carbohydrates.
Monday:
Breakfast: Porridge with mixed berries, honey, and chia seeds
Lunch: Tuna and sweetcorn sandwich on wholegrain bread, with a side of carrot and cucumber sticks
Dinner: Grilled salmon, roasted sweet potatoes, and steamed broccoli

Snack: Greek yogurt with granola and a drizzle of honey

Tuesday:
Breakfast: Scrambled eggs on whole grain toast with a side of avocado
Lunch: Chicken and avocado salad with mixed greens, cherry tomatoes, and a balsamic vinaigrette
Dinner: Vegetable stir-fry with tofu, served over brown rice
Snack: Apple slices with almond butter

Wednesday:
Breakfast: Greek yogurt with sliced banana, walnuts, and a drizzle of honey
Lunch: Turkey and salad wholegrain wrap, with a side of mixed fruit
Dinner: Baked cod with quinoa, roasted Mediterranean vegetables, and a lemon herb dressing
Snack: Dark chocolate covered almonds

Thursday:
Breakfast: Smoothie with spinach, blueberries, banana, and almond milk
Lunch: Lentil and vegetable soup, served with a slice of wholegrain bread
Dinner: Wholegrain pasta with a tomato and vegetable sauce, topped with grated Parmesan cheese
Snack: Hummus with wholegrain pita bread and veggie sticks

Friday:

Breakfast: Overnight oats with mixed berries, chopped nuts, and a dollop of Greek yogurt
Lunch: Smoked mackerel and mixed bean salad with a lemon and olive oil dressing
Dinner: Grilled chicken with a sweet potato and kale hash, served with a side of green beans
Snack: Cottage cheese with pineapple chunks

Saturday:
Breakfast: Wholegrain toast with peanut butter and sliced banana
Lunch: Egg and cress sandwich on wholegrain bread, with a side of mixed fruit
Dinner: Vegetable curry with chickpeas, served over brown rice
Snack: Celery sticks with cream cheese and a sprinkle of sunflower seeds

Sunday:
Breakfast: Spinach, mushroom, and feta cheese omelette
Lunch: Roasted vegetable and quinoa salad with a lemon-tahini dressing
Dinner: Roast chicken with roast potatoes, mixed vegetables, and a side of homemade gravy
Snack: Fresh fruit salad with a dollop of Greek yogurt

Remember to encourage your student to drink plenty of water throughout the day and aim for a balanced diet with a variety of fruits, vegetables, lean proteins, and whole grains.

Healthy and nutrient-rich snack

Fresh fruit: Apples, bananas, berries, oranges, and grapes are all great options. They provide natural sugars for energy and a variety of vitamins and minerals.
Dried fruit and nuts: A mix of dried fruits like apricots, raisins, and cranberries with nuts such as almonds, walnuts, and cashews provides a good balance of nutrients, including healthy fats and fibre.

Greek yogurt with honey and mixed seeds: Greek yogurt is high in protein and calcium, while honey provides natural sweetness and seeds like chia, flax, and sunflower are rich in healthy fats and fibre.

Vegetable sticks and hummus: Carrot, cucumber, celery, and bell pepper sticks can be dipped in hummus, which is made from chickpeas and is a good source of protein and healthy fats.

Rice cakes or wholegrain crackers with toppings: Top rice cakes or wholegrain crackers with options such as natural peanut butter, avocado, or cottage cheese for a protein-packed snack.

Dark chocolate: Choose a chocolate with at least 70% cocoa content for a delicious treat packed with antioxidants.

Oatcakes with cheese: Pairing oatcakes with a small portion of cheese provides a good combination of complex carbohydrates and protein.

Edamame: Lightly salted edamame beans are a healthy and tasty snack, rich in protein and fibre.

Granola bars: Choose a low-sugar, whole grain granola bar with nuts, seeds, and dried fruit for a convenient and nutritious snack.

Smoothies: Blend fruits like berries, bananas, or mangoes with yogurt or milk, and add a handful of spinach or kale for an extra nutrient boost.

Popcorn: Air-popped popcorn is a low-calorie, high-fibre snack. Season with a little salt or some spices for added flavour.

Roasted chickpeas: Chickpeas are high in protein and fibre, and can be roasted with a variety of spices for a crunchy, satisfying snack.

Printed in Great Britain
by Amazon

21737679R00036